Best-Ever
Back-to-School
Activities

Fifty Winning & Welcoming
Activities, Strategies & Tips
That Save You Time & Get Your
School Year Off to a Sensational Start

Compiled by Elaine Israel

SCHOLASTIC
PROFESSIONAL BOOKS

New York • Toronto • London • Auckland • Sydney
Mexico City • New Dehli • Hong Kong • Buenos Aires

For Ginnie Schroder, Maria Castano, and
Marilyn Scala, innovative and caring teachers, who
always make the start of school a time of joy.

A Special Thanks to Joan Novelli, Meish Goldish,
and Mary Beth Spann
for their invaluable creative contributions.

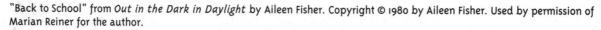

"Back to School" from *Out in the Dark in Daylight* by Aileen Fisher. Copyright © 1980 by Aileen Fisher. Used by permission of Marian Reiner for the author.

"First Day of School" from *I Wonder How, I Wonder Why* by Aileen Fisher. Copyright © 1962, 1990 by Aileen Fisher. Used by permission of Marian Reiner for the author.

"Hello Bus, Yellow Bus" from *101 Thematic Poems for Emergent Readers* by Mary Sullivan. Copyright © 1999 by Mary Sullivan. Used by permission of the author.

"I have two hands," "I have four legs," "I'm a fellow with a pointed head," "I'm covered with lines," "I take your books from home to school," "I'm rainbow colors," "Over my head," "I climb the ladder," "Draw the squares," "I'm 'it'," "Swoosh!," "Home run," "You use a racquet," "This ball is made of leather" from *201 Thematic Riddle Poems to Build Literacy* by Betsy Franco. Copyright © 2000 by Betsy Franco. Used by permission of the author.

"Leavetaking" from *It Doesn't Always Have to Rhyme* by Eve Merriam. Copyright © 1964, 1992 by Eve Merriam. Used by permission of Marian Reiner.

"New Friends" from *Month-by-Month Poetry: September, October & November* compiled by Marian Reiner. Copyright © 1999 by Patricia Hubbell. Used by permission of Marian Reiner.

"New Pencils" from *A Poem A Day* by Helen H. Moore. Copyright © 1997 by Helen H. Moore. Used by permission of the author.

"Old Friends, New Friends" from *25 Emergent Reader Plays Around the Year* by Carol Pugliano-Martin. Copyright © 1999 by Carol Pugliano-Martin. Used by permission of the author.

"School Tools" from *Month-by-Month Poetry: September, October & November* compiled by Marian Reiner. Copyright © 1999 by Monica Kulling. Used by permission of the author.

Cover design by **Norma Ortiz**

Cover artwork by **Amanda Haley**

Interior design by **BHG Graphic Designs**

Interior artwork by **Cary Pillo**

ISBN: 0-439-30462-8

Copyright © 2001 by **Scholastic Inc.**

All rights reserved.

Printed in the U.S.A.

Contents

Introduction

Welcome back to school! Getting the school year off to a good start is important for students and teachers alike. For you, it is a time to learn about students' abilities and interests. It's a time to initiate routines and set the tone for learning. For students it is an exciting time to meet new classmates, adjust to an unfamiliar environment, and discover what's in store for them in the year to come.

In this book you'll find a wonderful variety of learning-filled games, short plays, mini-books, bulletin boards, riddles, poems, and some back-to-school surprises. Turn to this book for fresh classroom-building ideas your students will love.

Here's hoping the year goes on as it begins—with excitement and academic success!

The First Day

Build community and establish routines with activities that will make the first day of school a stunning success.

Alumni Visits

To give your new students an idea of what the coming year will bring, invite a few of last year's students to visit your classroom and talk to the new class. Former students can tell about projects and activities they especially enjoyed, and provide some helpful hints.

Before the alumni arrive, ask the members of this year's class to prepare questions for their guests. For example: Did you think last year was hard? Why or why not? What did you most like doing all year? How did your class celebrate holidays? What advice would you give us for having fun this year?

After the former students have spoken to the class, open up the session for questions and answers.

"Good Morning" Match

Each child's cubby holds a welcoming surprise with an activity that makes it easy for new classmates to meet one another or get reacquainted and share a favorite book.

1. Cut construction paper in fun shapes. Stars are easy and appealing. Hand shapes are fun, too. Make one for each child.
2. On each cutout, write the name of a book that is part of your classroom collection. Write the same title on two cutouts to make pairs.
3. Punch a hole at the top of each cutout and string yarn to make a necklace.
4. Before the morning of the first day of school, place a necklace in each child's cubby.
5. Let children find their cubbies and put on the necklaces. Invite them to mingle with their classmates to find the person wearing a matching necklace. Have children say "good morning" to their partners, then find the book and look at it together.

Monster . . .

*T*his community-building activity brings children together for some monstrous fun, encouraging teamwork, and appreciation of differences.

You Need

- arts and crafts supplies
- clean milk cartons
- cardboard tubes
- egg cartons
- other recycled materials

1. Divide the class into small groups.

2. Provide each group with materials. Invite each group to use the materials to build a monster. The great thing about monsters is, of course, that they can have five arms or ten heads. This means that children can concentrate on having fun together, not on who is doing what.

3. Ask students to name their monsters, then introduce their creature to the class. Display monsters around the room. Children will enjoy hearing you refer to them from time to time. For example, as you discuss a story, you might ask, "What do you think Monster Max would say about what happened?"

What's Inside?

*W*hat could be more welcoming than a first-day gift, wrapped in bright paper and tied with a big bow? Inviting children to wonder what's inside is an engaging activity all by itself. Start by planning a simple gift for your new students—for example, a snack to share, a new book to read aloud, a puzzle to solve, a special sticker or certificate for each child, or a big box full of bright, new markers for the class.

Wrap the gift in a box that is just the right size. Display the box where children will easily see it when they enter the room. As the buzz begins about who it's for and what's inside, ask children to write down (or dictate) their guesses. Encourage them to share their reasoning, too. Discuss different ideas. What could fit inside? What couldn't? After allowing plenty of time for the suspense to build, slowly unwrap the gift and share it.

Calendar Surprise

A surprise awaits your students each day with this easy-to-make lift-the-flap calendar. Introduce the calendar on the first day of school. Children will look forward to calendar time every day as they wonder what's waiting for them under each flap.

1. Cut 16 pieces of 9-inch-by-12-inch construction paper in half, horizontally. You now have 32 pieces, one for every day of the month and more.

2. Fold each piece of construction paper in half and attach to a bulletin board or tagboard in a lift-the-flap calendar format. Be sure to label the name of the month and the days of the week on the calendar.

3. Write the dates on the outside of each square, and place a surprise under each calendar flap. You might write a riddle or joke, clues for finding another kind of surprise in the classroom, the title of a special book you're going to share, or a fun challenge—for example, "Find five things that start with the first letter of your name." You might also include fun stickers and mini-coupons, such as "Good for one extra recess" or "Good for one lunch with your teacher."

4. To keep students from peeking, seal flaps with colorful stickers or tacks.

5. Invite a child to find and say the date, then lift the flap and share the surprise with the class. Repeat the procedure each day, letting everyone take a turn sharing the daily surprise.

Create new lift-the-flap calendars for each month to keep the fun going all year. Your students can help create them. Just set up the calendars at a work station, and have children take turns adding the surprise under each flap. You might choose themes for each month. For example, October might be Halloween jokes and riddles to share. In honor of Children's Book Week, November's calendar might feature lift-the-flap clues about favorite books.

Classroom Discoveries

At the beginning of the school year, children will want to investigate all the nooks and crannies of your classroom.

Scavenger hunts are perfect ways to introduce children to their room, the school, and, of course, to one another. Here are three ways to do that.

1. Distribute the Classroom Treasure Hunt reproducible on page 9. Challenge each student to write at least one answer on every line.

   When students are done, have them share their answers with the class. You'll be amazed at the variety of items they come up with.

2. The Find Someone . . . grid on page 10 invites interactions among all the children in the class and will help students find out all sorts of interesting facts about one another.

After you give each child a copy of the grid, allow the children to mingle, looking for classmates who fit each description.

Have children sign one another's record sheets in the appropriate places. As a challenge, children can sign only once per sheet.

3. Use the All About Us survey on page 11 to help you graph students' likes and dislikes. Collect the sheets, and ask students to help you graph the "yes" answers. You could set up the graph the way it is shown on this page.

All About Us Tally

	LIKES PIZZA	HAS A PET	PLAYS SOCCER	LIKES PUZZLES	READS
10					
9	Jenny			Maria	
8	James			Sam	
7	Ryoko		Kelli	Josué	
6	Luke		Sam	Ryoko	Josué
5	Sally		James	Bella	Maria
4	Norma	Norma	Peter	Sam	Luke
3	Josué	Rachel	Colin	Peter	Jenny
2	Maria	Peter	Norma	André	Sally
1	Sam	Sally			
KIDS					

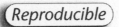

Name: _____

Classroom Treasure Hunt

On the lines, describe what you've found in the classroom.

Find something made of wood.

_____

Find something made of plastic.

_____

Find something made of metal.

_____

Find something taller than you.

_____

Find something shorter than you.

_____

Find something that starts with
the letter *n*.

_____

Find something that is green.

_____

Find something that has corners.

_____

Find something that has wheels.

_____

Find something you can see through.

_____

Find something that hangs.

_____

Find something that locks.

_____

Find something too heavy for you
to lift.

_____

Find something that snaps.

_____

Name: _____

¡hola!

Find Someone . . .

Fill in the name of a classmate in each box that describes that child.

who flew in an airplane over the summer	who discovered a secret place	who learned a new sport	who met a new friend
_____	_____	_____	_____
whose middle name starts with the letter *D*	whose birthday is in the same month as yours	who read more than five books this summer	who has one brother and one sister
_____	_____	_____	_____
who has a fish for a pet	who has a dog for a pet	who has a cat for a pet	who can speak a language other than English
_____	_____	_____	_____

Name: _____

All About Us

Choose a classmate to interview.
Write his or her answers on the blank lines.

I spoke to: _____

Do you like pizza? _____

Do you have a pet? _____

Do you play soccer? _____

Do you like to do puzzles? _____

What is your favorite kind of weather? _____

What is your favorite zoo animal? _____

What is your favorite color? _____

What is your favorite food? _____

What is your favorite book? _____

Getting to Know You

What better way for your students to identify one another's names and interests than fun-filled activities that get them reading, writing, singing, and learning!

Line for Line from A to Z

As a class, brainstorm words that begin with each letter. Then, invite your students to develop sentences like the ones listed at right. Help the children make torso-sized letter cards that they can wear around their necks. When you've completed this activity, display the alphabet cards for year-round reference.

Possible lines:

A is for apple.
B is for best.
C is for cat.
D is for dog.
E is for everyone.
F is for friends.
G is for great.
H is for happy.
I is for ice.
J is for jam.
K is for kindergarten.
L is for love.
M is for Monday.
N is for no.
O is for over.
P is for party.
Q is for quick.
R is for rush.
S is for Saturday and Sunday.
T is for Tuesday and Thursday.
U is for under.
V is for video.
W is for Wednesday.
X is for xylophone.
Y is for yesterday.
Z is for zoo.

Old Friends, New Friends

Use this mini-play as an icebreaker. To give as many children as possible speaking parts, have more than one child read or recite each of the lines.

Characters

Friends 1 to 8

Friend 1:   Do you like your old friends?

Friend 2:   Shy friends, bold friends, how we love our old friends!

Friend 3:   Sweet friends, neat friends, walking down the street friends.

Friend 4:   Good friends, glad friends, help you when you're sad friends.

Friend 5:   How about some new friends?

Friend 6:   New friends, true friends, lots of things to do friends.

Friend 7:   Hey, friends! Hello, friends! It's great to know you friends.

Friend 8:   Near friends, far friends, we're so glad we have friends!

Rebus Name Tags

Go beyond writing your name on the board for students to learn. Help them remember it by creating a rebus. Let children try to make their own name tags with rebus puzzles. You might have them pair up so they can help each other out.

For example, *Mrs. Einhorn*
could be

You Make Mine, I'll Make Yours

Pair students to make name tags.

1. Provide index cards and assorted art supplies, and let children make tags for their partners. (Children can spell their names for their partners.)

2. Laminate the tags, punch two holes at the top, and string with yarn. Children can wear their tags around their necks, hanging them up on their coat hooks at the end of the day.

Sing That Name!

Your class might be interested to know that the composer Wolfgang Amadeus Mozart was writing music at the age of five! While your students may not be prepared to write symphonies, they are ready to create song lyrics about their names.

1. Select a student.

2. Have the class sing about his or her name to the tune of "Bingo."

   For example:
   There's someone special in our class,
   And Bobby is his name, oh!
   B-O-B-B-Y,
   B-O-B-B-Y,
   B-O-B-B-Y,
   And Bobby is his name, oh!

3. Continue singing verses until everyone's name has been spelled out in song.

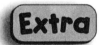

As a challenge, have the class clap hands instead of singing the first letter.

For example:
There's someone special in our class,
And Jane is her name, oh!
[CLAP] A-N-E,
[CLAP] A-N-E,
[CLAP] A-N-E,
And Jane is her name, oh!

Musical Name Chain

*Y*our students are sure to enjoy this musical activity designed to help them get acquainted with their classmates' names.

1. Ask your class to sit in a circle.

2. Choose one student (Maria, for example) to stand outside the circle. Then, have that child walk around the circle while everyone sings the following song to the tune of "The Farmer in the Dell":
   Maria's in the class,
   Maria's in the class,
   Hi-ho, the dairy-o,
   Maria's in the class

3. Maria then chooses someone to hold her hand and walk around the circle with her. The class sings:
   Maria chooses Deshawn,
   Maria chooses Deshawn,
   Hi-ho, the dairy-o,
   Maria chooses Deshawn

4. Deshawn then chooses someone to join him and Maria.
   Deshawn chooses Mark,
   Deshawn chooses Mark . . .

5. Continue the song and activity until all students in the class are holding hands and walking in a circle together.

Catch That Name

*G*et a soft rubber ball and gather students in a circle to play a get-to-know-you game. Start by giving one child the ball and asking him or her to throw or pass it to you. When you catch it, say the name of the person who threw you the ball, then say your name. Now, pass the ball to another student, and have that child say your name and his or her name. Continue until all children have caught the ball.

What's Your Name Worth?

*T*his double-fun activity helps students sharpen their math skills while they learn their classmates' names.

Write your students' names on the board along with the chart on page 17:

Mary = 57
Tom = 48
Meghan = 48
Paul =

1. Instruct each child to use the chart to figure out the price of his or her name. For example, the name PAUL would cost 16¢ + 1¢ + 21¢ + 12¢ = 50¢. Have each student write the amount next to his or her name on the board.

2. Then, pass out the reproducible on page 17 with these questions on it for students to answer.
Whose name costs the most?
Whose name costs the least?
Whose names cost less than 50¢?
Whose names cost more than 60¢?

Can you think of the names that would cost exactly 75¢?
What is the most expensive name you can think of?
What is the least expensive name you can think of?

Bonus

What makes a name cost more or less? (whether its letters fall toward the beginning or the end of the alphabet)

What's Your Name Worth?

Answer each of the questions. Use the chart to figure out your answers. Then, write them on the blank lines.

Meghan
13+5+7+8+1+14=
48

A	B	C	D	E	F	G	H	I	J	K	L	M
1¢	2¢	3¢	4¢	5¢	6¢	7¢	8¢	9¢	10¢	11¢	12¢	13¢

N	O	P	Q	R	S	T	U	V	W	X	Y	Z
14¢	15¢	16¢	17¢	18¢	19¢	20¢	21¢	22¢	23¢	24¢	25¢	26¢

Whose name costs the most? _____

Whose name costs the least? _____

Whose names cost less than 50¢? _____

Whose names cost more than 60¢? _____

Can you think of the names that would cost exactly 75¢? _____

What is the most expensive name you can think of? _____

What is the least expensive name you can think of? _____

Who Am I?

*I*n the game Mystery Classmate, the class tries to discover the secret identity of a fellow student. But in this version of the game, one student tries to discover his or her own identity—revealed to everyone else!

1. Prepare by having each child write his or her name in large letters on a strip of paper about 20 inches long and 6 inches high. Place all the names in a box.

2. Invite one student to come forward and pick a piece of paper without looking at the name on it. Tape it around the student's head so the name appears on his or her forehead for the whole class to read.

3. The student then tries to guess whose identity is on the headband by asking only "yes" or "no" questions.

> **Am I a girl?**
> **Do I have dark hair?**
> **Do I wear glasses?**
> **Am I tall?**

4. When the student thinks she knows her secret identity, she may take a guess. If she guesses incorrectly three times, reveal the answer. Then, call another student to wear a different headband.

Names by the Dozens

*F*rom cubbies to folders and the papers inside, all sorts of things need name tags. Here's a quick and easy solution that builds students' name-writing skills at the same time. At the beginning of the year, give each student a sheet of stick-on name tags. Have children write their names on the tags and decorate them. (You could also do this on the computer using a program like Kid Pix and printing on labels.) File the name tags you don't use right off the bat, and dip into them as the need arises—for example, use them to label bulletin-board projects and portfolios.

Birthday Time Line

Children won't have trouble remembering their own birthdays but they may have trouble recalling the birthdays of their classmates. You can solve this problem by creating a Birthday Time Line.

1. Give each student a sheet of white or light-colored construction paper. Tell each of your students to write his or her date of birth (month and day only) at the top of the paper and at the bottom of the paper, his or her name. Then have the children fill the rest of the page with a drawing. The picture might show a birthday gift they once received or would like to receive.

2. Collect all the papers, and ask your students to help you arrange them in chronological order. String a rope across the room, and clip the papers to the rope in that order. Now all of your students' birthdays are where everyone can see them! Each week or month, assign a birthday monitor to remind the class when someone's birthday is approaching.

September 9—Joe
October 13—Alan
November 4—Terri

It's a Puzzle

*T*ake photos of groups of ten children. Paste the photos on poster board, and write the children's names on the back. Cut the poster board into irregularly shaped pieces, making a jigsaw puzzle. Let each group work on another group's puzzle, trying to put the pieces together, familiarizing themselves with their classmates' faces and names as they work.

Add on to the Story

*T*ry this add-on story activity! Begin by writing the first sentence of a story on a sheet of notebook paper. For example: *Once upon a time, two birds named Toby and Lily were building a nest together, when a strong wind began to blow.* Pass the paper to the student nearest you in the classroom. Instruct him or her to read the sentence and then add a sentence to the story. Have that student pass the story to a neighbor, who adds a sentence, and so on. Caution students not to finish the story until it reaches the last person in the room, who provides an ending. When the story is completed, read it aloud to the class. Then, put it in your class library!

Pass the Popcorn

*P*ass around a bowl of popcorn or small pretzels. Ask children to wait until you say it's okay to eat the snack. After they take some, have children count the pieces of popcorn (or pretzels) in their hands. One at a time, invite children to tell about themselves—sharing one thing for each piece of popcorn they have. (For example, a child with eight pieces of popcorn will tell eight things.) To take the idea further, record children's comments on chart paper, one child per page. Put the pages together and bind to make a class book of mini-autobiographies.

Personality Bags

*A*t the beginning of the school year, it's a good idea to learn a little something about each student—and Personality Bags are a great way to do that! Ask your students to bring in grocery bags with five things inside that tell about themselves. The items might be favorite toys, books, articles of clothing, and/or photos. Then have each student make a brief presentation, explaining why each item is in the bag. A typical presentation might be:

> **"This is a picture of my dog. I walk him every morning and evening. This is a can of tuna, which is my favorite kind of sandwich. This is a baby rattle, because my mother just had a baby boy. This is a baseball. I was on a champion baseball team last summer. And this is an old sneaker, because I loved wearing it before it got too small."**

Allow time for class questions at the end of each presentation. You may want to share your own bag with students, too!

Bish Bosh

*B*ring children together in a circle. Have one child begin by pointing to another child and saying either "bish" or "bosh." If this child says "bish," the child whom he or she pointed to must tell the name of the classmate to the left. If this child says "bosh," the child he or she pointed to tells the name of the classmate to the right. The child who was pointed to takes over, pointing to another child and saying "bish" or "bosh." The game continues until all children have had a chance to name a classmate.

This is a good time to review left and right.

Who's the Leader?

*H*ere's a great way to let every student lead.

1. Have your children stand in a circle, and ask one to leave the room. While that student is out, designate a group leader. Tell your students to follow whatever movements the group leader makes, such as clapping hands, bobbing the head, wagging the tongue, or patting the head.

2. Now, ask the absent student to return to the classroom and stand in the middle of the circle.

3. Have the group leader make a movement, while the others imitate it. Every 15 seconds or so, the leader should begin a new movement. Have the student in the middle try to guess who the leader is. If that student fails to identify the leader after three guesses, reveal the answer.

4. Then play another round with a different leader and guesser.

Class Rhymedown

*I*f your class is not in a singing mood, the children are probably in a rhyming mood. So why not hold a rhymedown?

A rhymedown is similar to a singdown, except that teams must come up with rhyming words instead of song lyrics. For example, if the category were "words that rhyme with cheese," one team might say "please." The next team might say "sneeze." Other words to follow might include *breeze, trees,* and *freeze.* (Nonsense words are not acceptable.) A team is eliminated from the round if it can't think of a new rhyme, or if it accidentally repeats a rhyme.

There are endless categories you can provide for this game. Simply announce, "The category is words that rhyme with _____," and use any of the words below.

face	car	cheese	nice
back	chair	meet	quick
add	art	bed	hide
grade	cat	bee	bill
bag	late	near	pin
mail	gave	bell	nine
rain	saw	ten	pink
lake	ball	end	might
came	day	her	joke
pan	week	yes	tone
hand	dream	bet	broom
lap	clean	blue	chop
for	nose	dot	sound
low	boy	rough	sum
done	cup	day	mile

Mini-Books

When introducing **mini-books,** it is helpful to create a completed sample to share with your students. By reading through your book and pointing out all the steps you took, you help children feel comfortable when they create their own mini-books.

The following books have been designed for ease of assembly. Assemble the books together as a class, or depending on the level of your children, assemble the books yourself.

Making Books

Your students may want to bring these
delightful mini-books home to read again and again,
to themselves and their families.

How to Assemble the Books

Begin by making copies of the mini-book you would like to use. Keeping the pages faceup, invert every other page. Place the pages in your photocopier and make one double-sided copy of the mini-book for each student. Then, show your students how to assemble the mini-books by following these steps:

1. Put the pages in order by placing page B faceup on top of page A.
2. Fold the pages in half along the dotted line, making a little book.

3. Check to be sure that all of the pages are in the proper order. Then, staple them together along the book's spine.

4. Once the mini-book is assembled, it is time to invite your students to color the pictures and read the mini-book!

School Bells Ring Mini-Book

*T*alk about the changes from summer vacation to back-to-school routines. Ask: What was different in your home this morning compared with before school started? Was your bedtime last night earlier or later than your bedtime before school started? Did you feel different this morning than you did in the summer?

Invite children to note what else has changed or not changed in their daily routine and lifestyle. Make a chart comparing things that are different and things that are the same.

You may choose to elaborate on these topics:

- forming possessive nouns (such as "My teacher's name is _____")

- comparing and contrasting (favorite/least favorite)

- deciding what makes something special

School Bells Ring

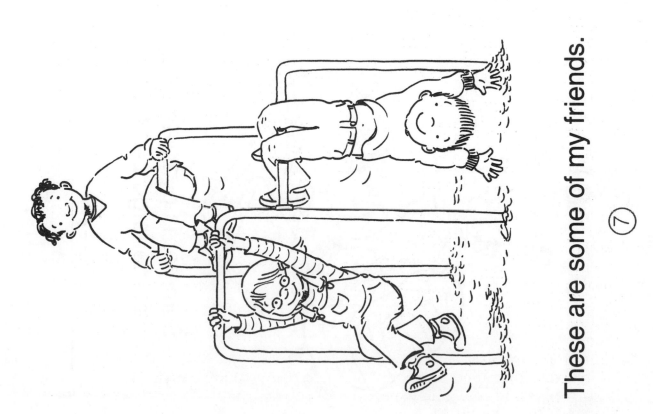

These are some of my friends.

⑦

In school I am looking
forward to

 6

Fold Here (A)

Summer is over, and
it is time to go back to

 1

This year I am in

_____

②

My teacher's name is

_____

⑤

My favorite part of school is _____

Fold Here ⑧

In school we learn to _____

and _____

So Long, Summer!

Hello to new friends.
Welcome to school!

⑦

Hello to books.

Fold Here

(A)

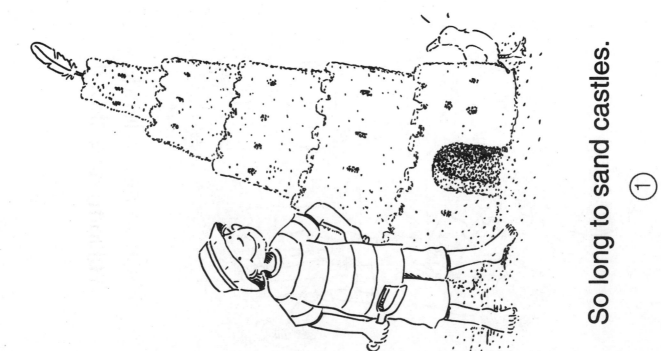

So long to sand castles.

①

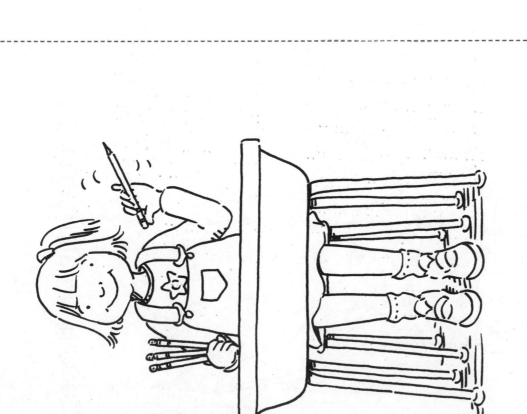

So long to seashells.

②

Hello to pencils.

⑤

So long to fireflies.

④

So long to watermelon.

③

Time for School

My Own List of New Things

⑦

new crayons

6

Fold Here

A

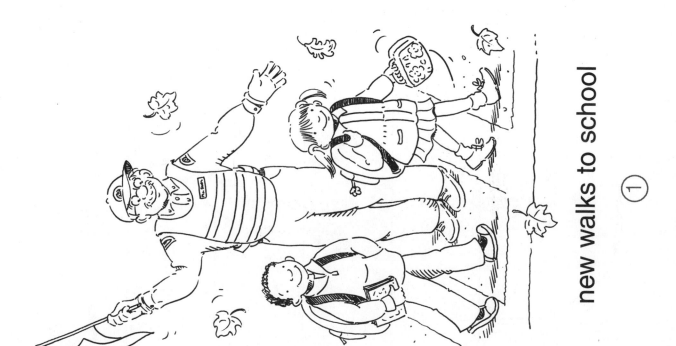

new walks to school

1

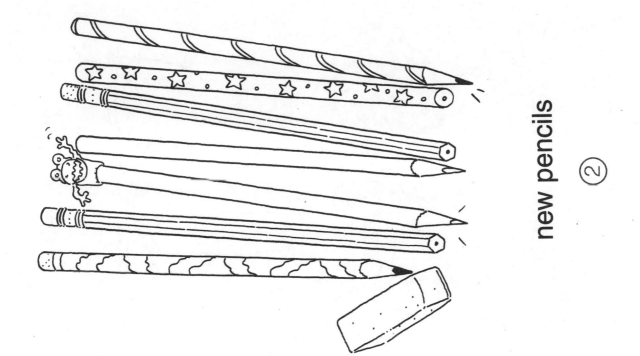

new pencils

② 2

new shoes

⑤ 5

new friends

④

Fold Here

Ⓑ

new teacher

③

Best Friends

But best of all, best friends
share time with each other.

⑦

Best friends share presents.

⑥

Fold Here

Ⓐ

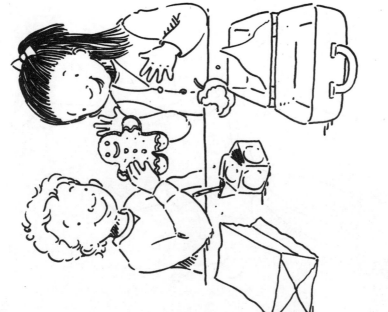

Best friends share cookies.

①

Best friends share stories.

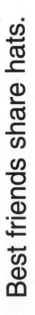

②

Best friends share hats.

⑤

Best friends share books.

④

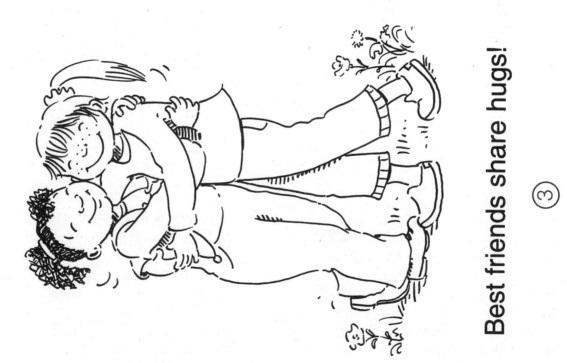

Best friends share hugs!

③

Collaborative Book
Back to School

Copy the poem "Back to School" (page 43) onto chart paper or sentence strips (for display in a pocket chart) and read it aloud with the class.

Back to School

Back to school—here I come!

A fresh new year of learning fun.

So many things to think and do!

I can't wait to _____ it's true!

*T*alk with your class about all the fun things they are looking forward to learning and doing this year in school. Ask children to think about what word(s) they would place in the blank to complete the poem. Give each child a copy of the poem on page 43. Read it through again. Have each child fill in the blank by writing or dictating his or her idea to you. The rest of the space on each page can be used for the children's illustrations of their idea.

To make the book cover, trace the schoolhouse pattern from page 42 onto red oak tag. Use a black marker or black puff paints to outline the schoolhouse shape and details. Color the schoolhouse bell with yellow marker or a bit of gold glitter glue. Cut open the schoolhouse doors and window shutters, and bend them open slightly to give the cover a 3-D effect. Use a hole punch to punch holes in the book pages and cover. Then, bind them together with brass fasteners. Display your book in your room, then circulate it among students' families.

Back to School

Back to school—here I come!

A fresh new year of learning fun.

So many things to think and do!

I can't wait to _____ it's true!

Bulletin Boards

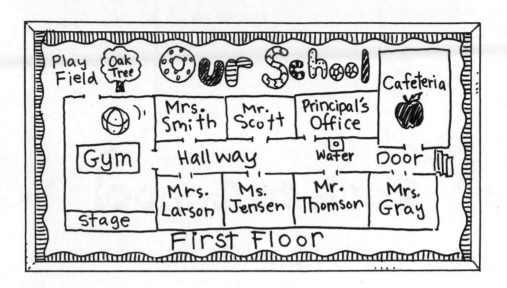

Class-Created School Map

You Need

6 craft paper

6 markers or crayons

*F*or new students, the school building is like a strange land. Create a big map to help them find their way around.

1. Divide the class into groups and assign each group a different floor or area of the building to map out.

2. Begin with a walking tour of the building. Point out all the rooms you pass and ask questions along the way to keep your students' attention focused. For example: What room is between the principal's office and the gym? How many classrooms are on this floor? If you walk left from Room 106, which office will you come to first?

3. Back in the classroom, give each group of students a large sheet of craft paper on which to draw each portion of the map. Students may first want to first draw a rough draft on a small piece of paper. Piece together the work of each group and place the entire school map on a wall. Refer to it all year long.

Getting to Know You

You Need

◎ pushpins

◎ one envelope for each child

◎ Leave notes for your students and they'll respond to you with their own notes.

Monday

On the bulletin board, attach an envelope for each student with his or her name on it. Inside the envelope, leave a short note about yourself. For example, you might write: Dear_____, I like to make my own kites and fly them. What things do you like to do? Your teacher, _____

Tuesday

Have children write notes in response. The notes should be placed in the students' envelopes.

Wednesday

Write a second note to each student, telling about an upcoming class activity. For example, you might write: Dear _____, This week we will be making leaf rubbings as a science project. What else would you like to do in class this year? Your teacher, _____

Thursday

Have children respond to the notes, and leave the responses in their envelopes.

Friday

Read aloud some of the letters you receive. Discuss your students' hobbies or the activities they would like to do as a class.

Graph It

You Need

⊚ craft paper

⊚ index cards

⊚ markers

⊚ photos of children

⊚ glue

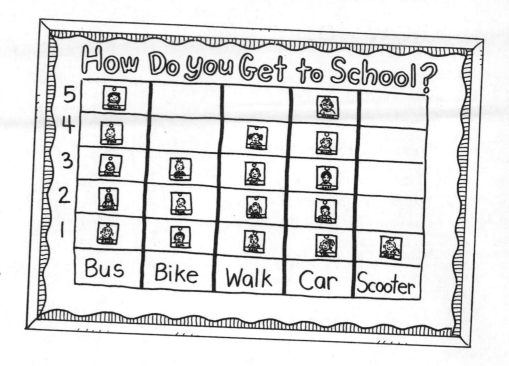

Draw a grid on a large piece of poster board or paper, and display it on a bulletin board. The dimensions will depend on the size of the board.

1. Mount a picture of each child in your class on an index card, and laminate it. Trim each card to fit inside the boxes on the grid, which will be used as the base of this board throughout the year.

2. Display a question above the graph, such as, What type of transportation do you use to get to school? Ask questions about current events, holidays, or your curriculum, for example. The question can change every week or so.

3. Place an index card with a category written on it at the bottom of the graph in each grid. For example, cards could be labeled "bus," "walk," "bike," "car." Students post their pictures in the appropriate column.

4. When the graph is completed, use it as a basis for math questions, such as, How many students in this class ride the bus? Do more students walk than ride? Students not only have a visual point to refer to when working on math questions, but they also learn about bar graphs and how to make them.

Special Person

You Need

- craft paper
- sentence strips
- markers
- pushpins
- chart paper
- hole punch
- photos of children
- glue
- name tags

The basic elements of this board—chart paper and markers—don't change. Just set up the display, then every week or two when you're ready to spotlight a new student, change the photos, pictures, and other items that celebrate that child.

1. Tack a stack of chart paper to the board. Write "Tell us what you like about ____" on a sentence strip and display above the chart paper.

2. Have each child write his or her name on a sentence strip, decorate it, and trim. Punch a hole in each card. Use a pushpin to hang name tags above the sentence.

3. Make the first student selection a surprise, setting up the board when students are out of the room. Pin the child's name in place to complete the sentence, and display

photos and a colorful name tag. Let children take care of the rest, drawing and displaying pictures for the special person, writing comments on the chart, and so on.

4. When you're ready to feature different students, have a couple of volunteers glue pictures to chart paper and make a cover. Put the cover page together with the picture and comment pages to make a book for the child to keep.

Model essay writing by using comments the children recorded about a classmate. Show how the reasons or facts they give support the statement that the child is special. As a class, rewrite the comments to tell a cohesive story about the child.

Tie in children's literature, for example, *Sheila Rae the Brave* by Kevin Henkes (Greenwillow, 1987). Students might appreciate Sheila Rae's outgoing nature and Louise's quiet strengths.

Make a home–school connection by inviting parents to celebrate the ways their children are special. For each child featured, ask parents or another special adult in the child's life to send in a note about the child and what makes him or her special. Add the note to the board, and watch that child beam!

Fun with a Friend

You Need

- craft paper
- box of markers or crayons
- signs
- mirror
- pushpins
- hammer and hook or nail
- spring clips
- photos of children
- drawing paper pad

1. Cover the board with craft paper, and add a border.

2. Display a sign: "Fun with a Friend." Add a smaller sign beneath this that says, "I will look at me and draw what I see. I will look at you and draw you, too!"

3. Securely affix a mirror to the board. You will be able to hammer a picture-framing hook or a nail through most bulletin boards and into the wall behind.

4. Use nails or pins to attach two spring clips to the board next to the mirror. Space them to hold a pad of drawing paper. Place the pad of paper in the clips. Pin up an open box of crayons or markers.

5. Invite a pair of children to demonstrate the activity. Have one child look in the mirror and draw a self-portrait. Have that child then look at his or her partner and draw that child, too. Encourage children to notice the kinds of details that will enhance their drawings—hair and eye color, the shape of a smile, and so on. The second child can then choose another child from the class and repeat the process. Children can continue, taking turns as both models and portraits artists.

Tip

Make seasonal and holiday links. Plan activities to correspond with events in your school and community. For example, if your class or school gardens in the spring, set up a seed-sorting activity at the board. Glue or tape an assortment of seeds to index cards (one kind of seed per card). Form two large yarn circles on the board. Glue pieces of Velcro to the backs of the cards and to the board (inside the circles). Let children work in pairs to sort the seeds. (One can start each set and the other can try to guess the rule and continue sorting, or they can work together.)

Perfect Poems

Each of the poems that follow deals with a different aspect of the start-of-school season. Here are some ways to use them:

🌀 Read an appropriate poem at the beginning of each day for the first week or so. After you've read all the poems, ask each child to write one of his or her own.

🌀 Make copies of the poems, laminate them, and post them.

🌀 Copy the poems on poster paper, and ask volunteers to illustrate them.

Leavetaking

Vacation is over;
it's time to depart.
I must leave behind
(although it breaks my heart)

Tadpoles in the pond,
A can of eels,
A leaky rowboat,
Abandoned car wheels;

For I'm packing only
Necessities:
A month of sunsets
And two apple trees.

—*Eve Merriam*

Back to School

When the summer smells like apples
and shadows feel cool
and falling leaves make dapples
of color on the pool
and wind is in the maples
and sweaters are the rule
and hazy days spell lazy ways,
it's hard to go to school.

But I go!

—*Aileen Fisher*

Hello Bus, Yellow Bus

Hello bus, yellow bus,
Wait, wait, wait!

Hello bus, yellow bus,
I'm late, late, late!

Hello bus, yellow bus,
One minute more!

Hello bus, yellow bus,
Open up your door!

Hello bus, yellow bus,
Now, I'm on my way!

Hello bus, good-fellow bus,
You really saved the day!

—*Mary Sullivan*

First Day of School

I wonder
if my drawing
will be as good as theirs.

I wonder
if they'll like me
or just be full of stares.

I wonder
if my teacher
will look like Mom or Gram.

I wonder
if my puppy
will wonder
where I am.

—*Aileen Fisher*

New Friends

This morning, when
I started school,
I met a girl
named Betty Lou
and she met me—
That made us *two*.

Then, both of us
met Anne Marie—
And that made *three*.

Then, Paul came running
through the door—
Now, the three of us
are *four*—
And I can't wait to meet some more!

—*Patricia Hubbell*

Schools Tools

I like the look
of my new clean book,
of my pencils six
like pick-up sticks.

I like my eraser
smelling of pink,
wiping mistakes
and helping me think.

I like my ruler
straight as a line
and scissors that cut
paper so fine.

But I like my lunchbox
best of all,
walking to school
in the crisp, new Fall.

—*Monica Kulling*

New Pencils

Long and thin
with pointed tops
waiting in my
pencil box—
Yellow pencils,
(Number 2)
Do just what
I tell them to—
They can draw
both straight and wavy,
Draw one boat,
or draw a navy!
(Even draw French fries with gravy!)
New pencils, I love you!

—*Helen H. Moore*

A Song to Sing

Note to Teachers:
End your first day or first week of school on
a cheerful note by having a community sing-along.
Make copies of this song.

- -

Sharing, Caring Friends
(sung to the tune of "Camptown Races")

What is fun for friends to do?
Sharing! Caring!
Who am I and who are you?
Sharing, caring friends!
I like you, and you like me,
Sharing! Caring!
It's the nicest thing to be,
Sharing, caring friends!

CHORUS:
Being a friend all day,
Being a friend all night.
Whether times are glad or sad,
Friends will make them right!

Share your dog, I'll share my cat,
Sharing! Caring!
Share your ball, I'll share my bat,
Sharing, caring friends!
Share your peach, I'll share my plum,
Sharing! Caring!
Share your horn, I'll share my drum,
Sharing, caring friends!

CHORUS

Riddle Poems

Want to make students smile? Turn to some wonderful riddle poems from Betsy Franco's *201 Riddle Poems to Build Literacy* (Scholastic, 2000). Read them aloud, and enjoy your students' giggles. Or copy them onto sentence strips, and tuck them in a pocket chart.

Tip

Extend this activity by having students write a paragraph or two about each object or activity—from the point of view of the pencil or jump rope, for example.

What Can You Find in the Classroom?

I have two hands. I have a face.
My hands go round and round.
I have the numbers 1 to 12
instead of smiles and frowns.
Find me in the classroom.

Answer: *clock*

I have four legs.
I'm made from a tree.
You stuff your books
inside of me.
Find me in the classroom.

Answer: *desk*

I'm a yellow fellow with a pointed head.
As thin as thin can be.
But I leave a trail on a blank white page
when someone writes with me.
Find me in the classroom.

_____

Answer: *pencil*

I'm covered with lines,
and I'm most often white.
I'm handy when
you want to write.
Find me in the classroom.

_____

Answer: *paper*

I take your books from home to school.
I'm red or blue or green or black.
You zip my zippers here and there.
I'm always riding piggyback.
Find me in the classroom.

_____

Answer: *backpack*

I'm rainbow colors
like red and blue.
When you draw or color,
I'm what you use.
Find me in the classroom.

_____

Answer: *crayon*

What Am I Playing?

Over my head
and under my feet,
The rope twirls around,
as I jump to the beat.
What am I doing?

_____

Answer: *jumping rope*

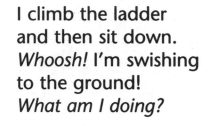

I climb the ladder
and then sit down.
Whoosh! I'm swishing
to the ground!
What am I doing?

_____

Answer: *sliding on the slide*

Draw the squares
in white or black.
Throw a stone.
Hop up and back.
What am I doing?

_____

Answer: *playing hopscotch*

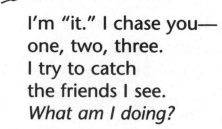

I'm "it." I chase you—
one, two, three.
I try to catch
the friends I see.
What am I doing?

_____

Answer: *playing tag*

Balls: Which Sport?

Home run,
single, double, too.
You hit this ball
and catch it, too.
It's a _____.
Answer: *baseball*

You use a racquet
to hit this ball.
It's yellow or white,
and fuzzy and small.
It's a _____.
Answer: *tennis ball*

Swoosh!
It's going through the hoop.
The happy crowd
lets out a *whoop*.
It's a _____.
Answer: *basketball*

This ball is made of leather—
partly white and partly black.
You try to get in the goal.
You kick it up and back.
It's a _____.
Answer: *soccer ball*

Top Ten
Start-of-the-Year
Stories

**Books are always
a wonderful way
to bring students
together.**

With all of the anxiety, excitement, and other emotions that often come with the first days of school, what could be more welcoming, more comforting than a good read-aloud? Treat your students to the treasures that follow. To make the first book you read aloud to students an extra-special treat, wrap it up and tie with a big bow. What a great gift!

Top Ten Start-of-the-Year Stories

Tip

Many of Kevin Henkes's books have reassuring messages for young children. **Owen** (*Greenwillow, 1993*) and **Wemberly Worried** (*Greenwillow, 2000*) are two other excellent choices for the start of the school year.

Chrysanthemum
by Kevin Henkes
(*Greenwillow, 1991*)

Chrysanthemum is a confident young mouse. But her confidence is shaken when she starts school and her classmates make fun of her name: "It's so long." "It scarcely fits on your name tag." "You're named after a flower." Chrysanthemum isn't sure school is the place for her. But when the other children learn that their beloved music teacher's name is Delphinium (and she's considering naming her new daughter Chrysanthemum), everything changes.

Your students might like to count and compare letters in their own names. What is the shortest name? the longest? (See page 16 for a related activity.) Use the book as a springboard to community-building activities that help children appreciate ways they are alike and different.

Emily's First 100 Days of School
by Rosemary Wells
(*Hyperion, 2000*)

Cheerful illustrations welcome young readers into Emily's classroom, where she starts the year by exploring the number *1*.

Make a class book about your students' first day by having each child complete the following sentence from the story: On the first day of school, I  _____ . Place children's illustrated pages together to make a book. Let them take turns sharing the book at home.

Lunch Bunnies

by Kathryn Lasky

(Little Brown, 1996)

Clyde is feeling confident about his first day of school—about everything, that is, except lunch. His older brother fuels his fears. "You better hope they don't have soup," he tells Clyde. Or mystery goosh. Clyde worries all morning, but he makes it through the lunch line. There's no soup and no mystery goosh. But there is Jell-O—cut into little cubes that go boing-boing when they spill off a classmate's tray and onto the floor. This funny turn of events will help young readers master their own first-day fears and look forward to the new friends they can make in the process.

For a fun confidence-building follow-up, borrow some trays from the cafeteria. Let children put pretend food on them and practice carrying them from one end of the room to the other.

This Is the Way We Go to School

by Edith Baer

(Scholastic, 1992)

Some children walk, ride bikes, or take a bus to school. Others take a ferry, a vaporetto, even a helicopter! Travel the world with this book to learn about the many ways children get to school.

After sharing the story, make a human graph—with children lining up by the way they get to school. Have the first child in each line hold a picture of that form of transportation.

I Spy School Days:
A Book of Picture Riddles
by Jean Marzollo and Walter Wick
(Scholastic, 1995)

Children flock to books in the I Spy series and will be delighted to find this one waiting for them. Use the picture on pages 8 and 9 as inspiration for a class I Spy interactive display that also teaches the letters of the alphabet. Start by letting children explore the picture, finding and naming objects for each letter of the alphabet. Then, make a class interactive I Spy alphabet display. Assign each child (or pair of children) a letter. Have children form their letters out of clay and arrange them in alphabetical order on a table. Then, have them gather objects (or pictures) for their letters. Let children display the objects in random order around the letters. Together, write riddles about the letters and objects. Invite other classes to visit your I Spy display to solve the picture riddles.

The Secret Shortcut
by Mark Teague
(Scholastic, 1996)

If you have any students who are not quite sure school is the place they want to be, share this wacky story to take their minds completely off their troubles. They'll meet Wendell and Floyd, who just can't get themselves to school on time. If it's not aliens keeping them, it's pirates or frogs. Wendell and Floyd's frustrated teacher gives them one last chance. "Be here on time tomorrow—or else! And no more crazy excuses!" she tells them. Their foolproof shortcut, sure to get them there on time, takes them over the fence and . . . into their wildest adventure of all!

Tip

Have fun after the story by letting children take turns telling the wildest excuses they can think of for being late to school.

Someone I Like
(Barefoot Books, 1999)

This book of poems is filled with tiny treasures that will inspire friendships among new classmates.
Share Nikki Giovanni's "Two Friends" for starters. Let students share things they have in common with their friends. Follow up by using the poem as a model for students' own poems about friends.

There's a Zoo in Room 22
by Judy Sierra
(Harcourt, 2000)

When the idea of getting a class pet comes up—and it's bound to—share this story about a teacher who responds by offering her students a whole alphabet of pets. Rhyming text introduces a pet for each letter. There's Amanda Anaconda, Boring Beetle Bill, Claude the Cat, Our Dog Doug, and more. The book ends with an invitation for your students to come up with a pet for the letter Z.

Tip

The natural extension to this story, of course, is to have students collaborate on their own alphabet of pets. Have them write each letter and pet's name on a piece of tagboard and illustrate it. Display as an alphabet frieze for a classroom resource students will never tire of looking at.

Tip

Read the story, then give each child a star. Have children write (or dictate) safety tips on the stars (like the stars on the inside front cover of the book), then illustrate them. Let children share their stars, then add them to a safety display.

Officer Buckle and Gloria
by Peggy Rathmann
(Putnam, 1995)

Safety lessons are a natural for the start of the school year—and this is the book to get students thinking about safety in their school. In this exuberant Caldecott-Award winner, Officer Buckle shares safety tips with students. But they don't pay attention until his new canine pal, Gloria, comes along and livens things up.

Tip

Here's another opportunity for engaging open-ended questions. What would you do to make sure Jim has a friend? What have you done to make friends?

Will I Have a Friend?
by Miriam Cohen
(Simon & Schuster, 1967)

When Pa was taking Jim to school for the first time, Jim said, "Will I have a friend at school?" Pa reassures Jim that, yes, he will have a friend. There's a wagon of blocks, clay to pinch and pat, juice and cookies to share, but no friends to be found. Then at rest time, Paul quietly shows Jim his tiny truck. Jim offers to bring his gas pump the next day. And so the friendships begin. Still a favorite after more than thirty years, this quiet story will offer encouragement to any child with first-day fears. Don't be surprised if it inspires your students to make extra efforts to include one another.